I0437643

Fort Rules

Fort Rules
by
Richard A. Hollen

Illustrated
by
Julia Damion

iUniverse, Inc.
New York   Bloomington

Fort Rules
A Guide to Getting Along

Copyright © 2009 by Richard A. Hollen

All rights reserved. No part of this book may be used or reproduced by any means, graphic, electronic, or mechanical, including photocopying, recording, taping or by any information storage retrieval system without the written permission of the publisher or the author except in the case of brief quotations embodied in critical articles and reviews.

iUniverse books may be ordered through booksellers or by contacting:

iUniverse
1663 Liberty Drive
Bloomington, IN 47403
www.iuniverse.com
1-800-Authors (1-800-288-4677)

Because of the dynamic nature of the Internet, any Web addresses or links contained in this book may have changed since publication and may no longer be valid. The views expressed in this work are solely those of the author and do not necessarily reflect the views of the publisher, and the publisher hereby disclaims any responsibility for them.

ISBN: 978-1-4401-2660-4 (pbk)
ISBN: 978-1-4401-2661-1 (dj)
ISBN: 978-1-4401-2664-2 (ebk)

Library of Congress Control Number: 2009925388

Printed in the United States of America

iUniverse rev. date: 5/21/2009

The heart of any team is interpersonal relationships.

The heart of networking is interpersonal relationships.

The heart of business is interpersonal relationships.

Fort Rules is all about interpersonal relationships.

Gratitude

Fort Rules is dedicated to my wife, Kendra, who followed me to the four corners of the lower forty-eight states during seventeen years of military marriage, moved the same number of times in so many years, worried about me during the numerous deployments and exercises when she couldn't follow me, fixed the car, painted the house, chased the dog, mowed the lawn, drove children to the emergency room, and handled the plethora of life events that seemed to wait for me to leave before popping up. In all of this she seldom missed a day of writing me when I was away.

Kendra, my heart was always with you.

And if I don't mention Zachary, Rachel, Lydia, Moriah, and Augustin here, I'll soon find myself on the bottom of a six-person people-pile when they gang up on me. Needless to say, there would be no *Fort Rules* if there were no kids to build the fort.

Special thanks to my friends and editors Rachel Allison and Mary MacDonald Murray.

Above all, I thank God for the myriad of life events and experiences, good and bad, that have equipped me to write this book.

Contents

Preface

Whenever people in any group, gathered for whatever purpose, begin to bicker and squabble, some well-intentioned person will inevitably blurt out, "Why can't we all just get along?"

Most of this short book is an attempt to provide some guiding principles on *how to get along*—not from me, but from a gang of kids who played together in a fort of their own building and discovered that a few basic rules were necessary to help them get along.

The last chapter answers the opening question and explains why the simple guiding principles are so difficult to put into practice.

In 2006, I was appointed to a key leadership position in Baghdad for the reconstruction of Iraq. As a team, we accomplished extraordinary things under some of the most adverse circumstances—the success stories you do not read about in the mainstream media. However, for me it was the preceding twenty years of experience that set the stage for that success.

Leadership is a challenge, a burden, a blessing, and a curse all at the same time. The first lesson in military leadership I learned over twenty years ago, is that the leader is responsible for everything his or her people do or fail to do. Everything. That first lesson has been reinforced in my mind time and time again throughout my eclectic career. I've held numerous leadership and management positions, but never had the inclination to write a book on either subject (and they are different subjects); that is, until I read my kids' fort rules—ten rules, simple yet profound. I was amused at first and then gripped by them. When friends I shared the rules with reacted in a similar manner, I knew I had to write this book.

This book is short (as most of my favorites are). <u>Message to Garcia</u> by Elbert Hubbard has been my life-long "how-to" book—thirty-two pages. Will and Ariel Durant summarized what they learned in researching and writing their eleven-volume *Story of Civilization* in *Lessons of History*—eighty-nine pages.

When I was a young lad, listening to the weekly Sunday sermon, my favorite reverend was the one who said any minister who couldn't say his piece in twenty minutes wasn't worth listening to. I was sorely disappointed a few years later when I learned (one hour into his sermon) he had abandoned that philosophy.

If you are anything like me, your attention span has just about reached its limit, so turn the page.

Introduction

From March to September 2006 I was assigned to a military staff position in Baghdad, Iraq. During that period my wife wrote a letter nearly every day. With the modern technology of e-mail and VOIP phones, we corresponded often and managed all our routine business via the communication methods that offered us instant gratification, but I eagerly anticipated her letters. Having the routine business out of the way left ample opportunity for more personal thoughts to be penned in ink on old-fashioned paper. She regularly slipped a photo, cartoon, news clipping, or other item of interest into the envelope. It was in this manner that the kids' "fort rules" first came to me.

Immediately I got a kick out of reading the rules, maybe more so due to the fact that we were in the middle of a war. The thought struck me: *If we could all just follow these ten simple principles, maybe we wouldn't need to be here at all.*

I shared the page my wife had covertly photocopied from our children's secret "Fort Book" with my co-workers, and, after seeing they were equally amused, I did what every good desk jockey of the dot.com techno-era does—I scanned the document then sent it to everyone in my electronic address book! And thus, my friends, another e-mail chain was created. Some of the recipients forwarded the e-mail, and I soon began to receive e-mail replies commenting on the appropriateness of the "Rules."

Several people posted the "Rules" in their cubicles, work sections, or conference rooms. One office near the ancient ruins of Babylon officially adopted them to govern all their meetings.

I guess the point is, if children can conjure up some basic rules for getting along and agree to abide by them, might not those same rules be every bit as applicable in our adult relationships, meetings, work environments, and day-to-day interactions?

About the Fort

What do kids with ten acres of woods in a rural area do to entertain themselves when they are not busy with schoolwork or chores? They build forts! They build them out of anything they can get their hands on. They soon learn it is easier to beg forgiveness than to ask permission when scrounging for material. Even if they have professionally built swing sets, playgrounds, and tree houses, they will still build forts.

The fort at hand would not have looked like much to the ordinary passerby. In fact, I'm sure if most people had seen it in that remote corner of our yard, they would have muttered to themselves, "Why don't those people clean up that mess?"

It was a custom array of branches, rope, old barn doors painted blood red, a beekeeper's hive box, some plywood scraps, old fence rails, excess roofing panels, and—well, by now you should have the picture, which would be worth a thousand words, if only such a photograph existed. Unfortunately, the "mess" was eventually cleaned up. Although we often said, "We really should get the camera out and go take a picture of that thing," we never quite got around to it.

The fort totaled about eighty or ninety square feet, with individual rooms and an office. It had trap doors and secret entrances, escape routes and places for storing weapons. The fort was heavily defended by pinecone-chucking catapults made from plastic Coke bottles duct-taped to sapling trees.

At one time the fort boasted a second story, but I instituted a rule of my own—no one was allowed in the lower story whenever anyone was in the upper one (as the design and choice of building materials was, shall we say, a bit suspect).

In short, the fort was the pride and joy of the children of neighboring families—not because the fort was so *good* (at least not in the adult sense of the word), but because they, the children, had built it themselves.

The children then learned a difficult lesson about surveying when they were informed they had built their fort precisely on a property line. What had taken a couple years to perfect was reduced to nothing in a day. After several mostly peaceful protests, the fort was surrendered to accommodate a gravel driveway.

About the Kids Who Built the Fort

In many ways the kids of the fort were no different from other kids around the world. They went to school, they did homework, and they did occasional jobs around the house. When they were not working they were playing. Sometimes even play was work—building a fort, in this case.

A couple of kids—usually the older ones—naturally tended to be the leaders of the pack. Several followed the group and did whatever the others were doing. One, whose antics tended toward the mischievous side, may have been the reason for some of the "Rules."

The gang was a mix of boys and girls, but mostly girls. When not constructing or remodeling the fort they spent their time warding off pirates, slaying dragons, sword fighting with swords made of sticks and duct tape, or spying on the "big boys" in the next lot over.

But life is not all fun and games. Sometimes serious business takes precedence even in the lives of preteens. At such a time, a fort meeting was convened, and the kids soon discovered that a few rules were necessary to maintain order so that they could get down to business.

What follows is the list of the ten fort rules as they were inscribed in the kids' secret "Fort Book," with a grown-up exposition of each rule. Ironically, sometimes the things "so simple even children can do them" somehow prove to be quite difficult in the adult world.

Fort Rules

#1 Obey Leader at All Times

The first rule is a tough one. Obedience doesn't come naturally for most of us. We could go into a discourse about blind obedience or lawful orders, but since this is Number One in the minds of children, let's keep it simple.

In our society we practice *democracy*. We elect our leaders. The ones we vote for don't always win, but our voices are heard. We make choices about our employment, the schools we attend, the professors we take, and the people with whom we spend our lives.

Most of us find ourselves in some type of leadership position at some point in our lives, but being in a leadership position does not equate to being a leader.

Are the best leaders good followers first? Are some people natural-born leaders? Are leaders forged by training and circumstances? The answer to all the above is *yes*, at least most of the time, as there are exceptions to every rule.

| • **Lead by inspiration, not intimidation.** |

There are volumes written on leadership, leadership traits, leadership characteristics, leadership principles, leadership styles, and so on. There are some who lead by force or intimidation—the dictators—while others lead by inspiration. What is often overlooked is that leadership requires a lot of work and dedication.

There are those, both among the (so-called) leaders and those who are led who assert that leaders do very little else besides bark out commands, issue orders, and generally boss others around. While these bossy bosses no doubt exist, they are not leaders.

If there is one thing true leaders have in common, it is commitment to their causes and their followers. A leader committed to people and purpose will never lose sight of either, but at times may have to decide between the two. It takes people to achieve the purpose. This is why leadership by inspiration wins out over leadership by intimidation every time. A leader who inspires his people to share his vision and to desire the same purpose and to strive together toward the same goal, is infinitely more likely to achieve that end or goal with the unit, company, or team and relationships intact than the one who attempts the same by bossing people around.

Self-serving egotists will use and abuse others to further their own agendas, but a true leader is nearly as concerned (if not more so) with the well-being of those he leads as he is with what he accomplishes.

Leaders can manage things (time, budgets, schedules, stuff), but they lead people. As a leader, if you want people to obey or follow your lead, convince them that they want to do so. Show them you not only have a purpose in mind, but also care about them as people.

#2 No Bossing Higher Positions

No one likes a backseat driver. No boss will appreciate you charging into his office to tell him just how screwed up you think he is. No one with whom you are in a relationship will take kindly toward your imposing your will forcefully on him or her.

The previous chapter was directed toward leaders; this one is directed toward followers. If we are honest with ourselves, most of us have both leadership roles and following roles in our lives. Most of us have a boss, or a board, or a partner, or a teacher, or someone that we answer to in one capacity or another.

Unless we are of the most wishy-washy sorts, we do not always agree with those in authoritative positions over us. Most of us are thinkers and have ideas and opinions of our own. Some are more opinionated than others. Some are more vocal about expressing those opinions than others. Some are downright boisterous. Some are articulate and persuasive, while others rant and rave.

> ## • **Be persuasive, not pushy.**

Effecting change is never easy. There are volumes written on the subject and entire graduate level courses dedicated to change management. If you find that you are tempted to "boss the higher positions" it is probably because you are in disagreement with some policy, action, habit, decision, or something else, and you are seeking change in policies, actions, habits, etc.

The one who approaches the higher position, or anyone else for that matter, with a boisterous, bossy rant, will immediately put that person on the defensive. Not to mention, those who negotiate like this (and this is really what we are talking about, a negotiation for change of some sort) usually look foolish and rarely get their way.

> ## • **Tactfully approach others when seeking change or resolution.**

On the other hand, those who are able to tactfully articulate their position are often able to persuade the decision maker to see things from another perspective. Some of us who hold higher positions can admittedly be headstrong. We don't necessarily care if everyone sees life our way or not. What we want is conformity. In cases like this it may be necessary to articulate to the decision maker how another approach will benefit him in the short or the long run or both, and convince him you have his or the company's or the relationship's best interest at heart.

Being subtle, tactful, and articulate requires deliberate thought, which necessitates much more effort than ranting and raving, but if you want to effect a change and at the same time maintain your job or relationship, it is the only worthwhile approach.

#3 No Pestering or Threatening

Threats run a wide range from "I'll tell Mom!" to threats of serious violence and criminal acts. Serious threats, such as violence to oneself or others, should be taken seriously and the matter referred to professionals. These aside, however, most threats fall into the *pestering* or annoyance category—"I'll tell Mom," or, "I won't be your friend."

> • **Don't agitate or aggravate.**

No one needs to teach us how to be annoying—it's our nature. We inevitably do something, have some idiosyncrasy or habit, that annoys someone else. Others of us have turned pestering into an art form!

Every child, and anyone who has ever been a child, knows exactly what it is to pester or be pestered. Funny thing, though, no child likes to be the pesteree, but they all seem to enjoy being the pesterer.

We all have our pet peeves, and we all know how to find those of our fellow human beings. We always seem to know just what buttons to push. How is it, then, that when we know how much we hate to be annoyed we can be so oblivious when it comes to annoying other people? This brings us to a distinction we need to make: active vs. passive pestering.

Active pestering is a deliberate action taken to get under someone else's skin either for our own selfish gain (to elevate ourselves at the expense of someone else) or to the other person's detriment because we don't like that other person or because he is an easy target—the kid everyone teased in school. Since it's done intentionally, active pestering is easier to recognize, which is more than half the battle in ending it. Passive pestering is not quite so simple. It's passive because we don't even realize we are doing it. It's pestering because it annoys the _____ out of our spouses, friends, co-workers, the people near us in the shopping center—practically everyone.

What are these things? We all have them: chewing gum like a camel, starting every sentence with *like* and ending it with *you know*, not bathing often enough, snorting phlegm, singing the same phrase of the same song over and over, one-upping at every opportunity, asking too many questions, breaking the two-minute conversation rule, or constantly steering a conversation to one's own experiences—this list could go on and on.

Perhaps you've read the list and you paused at an item and thought *that's not so bad*. That could indicate you're guilty of that particular passive pestering and it's annoying the _____ out of everyone else. The point here is that we need to take personal inventories and do what we can about our own little annoying habits.

The flip side to this, you could argue, is for the majority (those so easily annoyed) to get a thicker skin or just practice a little more tolerance toward the annoying few. While there is a lot to be said on both points, a true friend could find a way to tactfully inform a spouse, co-worker, or even the boss about his or her pestering actions or habits, doing everyone a real favor and improving the working relationship at the same time— easier said than done. Most of us would prefer to continue just talking *about* the person and their annoying little habits.

• Don't manipulate.

Some threats take on a bit different form of pestering, in that they can cause considerable stress and angst. Think about the boss who threatens to withhold pay, benefits, recognition, or promotions, or to give a bad report as a means of manipulating employees. Think about employees who threaten to undermine their companies or supervisors because they can or because they don't like them or to assert their own self-worth in a negative way. What about the spouse who threatens to withhold favors, money, time, or gifts from a wife or husband in order to get his or her own way?

In each of these examples, the one who threatens is more concerned with getting or maintaining the upper hand in the relationship than they are with the relationship itself.

For those readers who tend toward the threatening side, I refer you back to Rule #1. Inspiration wins out over intimidation.

#4 No Throwing Objects

It's difficult to accomplish anything with a plethora of missiles being hurled through the room, whether by a wife throwing pots and pans at her inattentive husband, a co-worker winging a pen or stapler at an antagonist, or a boss (or employee for that matter) clearing a mahogany desktop with a single sweep of the arm. More often than not, the thrown objects are a good indication that the source is throwing a fit. Have you ever witnessed a toddler throwing a tantrum? Forks, food, toys, cups zing through the air, and the child looks completely foolish while embarrassed parents try everything in their power to console, distract, or redirect the insolent child. Well, tantrum throwing does not get prettier with age.

> • **Always maintain control over actions and emotions.**

Ranting and raving will get attention, probably a lot of it, but not usually the type of attention desired. A fit of rage indicates a severe loss of self-control. Think about this for a moment: how can we expect people to control the destiny of a Fortune 500 company, a third grade classroom, or a meeting of the board of deacons if they cannot control their own emotions or conform themselves to a few social norms such as not throwing objects when proper decorum dictates otherwise.

Those of us with hot tempers will not take kindly to being told we need to exercise a little self-control. We will blame others when we lose our composure and then send some object flying across the room—"they made me so angry." And when there is not a solitary other person we can reasonably blame, however remotely, we will in fact blame a "stupid" but inanimate object, quite often the one we've just thrown, like the hammer that just wouldn't strike the nail straight on, causing the nail to bend. After all, it could never be our own hammering skills that might require a little honing. That's absurd! It was the hammer's fault, and we are bewildered when the innocent onlookers look on half in shock. Certainly it's just as obvious to them that the hammer was defective and deserved to be thrown! In the process we've also likely thrown out a few choice expletives, but we'll address that under Rule #9.

Throwing objects in a fit of rage does little to endear us to our families and friends. If you want to alienate and isolate yourself from someone, throw an object at him or her. Throw a tantrum during a business transaction and you just might throw the deal.

#5 Stay in Seats at All Times During a Meeting

As a general rule, we can probably all agree that staying in our seats is conducive to the good order and conduct of a meeting in the conference room or a conversation at the kitchen table. There are some quite obvious exceptions to this rule. Certainly there are different leadership and briefing styles for which it is more appropriate for someone to stand. The situation will dictate that, but for the most part we conduct our meetings sitting in chairs at tables.

> • **Be attentive and courteous.**

It is distracting and disrespectful when those supposedly participating in the meeting are constantly up and down—out of their seats, going to the restroom, getting coffee, and the ultimate social *faux pas* of our era, texting and taking cell phone calls. Again, there are exceptions and the situation should dictate proper manners. Better to excuse yourself to use the restroom than to pee yourself. Better to stand and get coffee than to fall asleep drooling on the table, and occasionally a cell phone call is related to the meeting purpose and the information in the call will facilitate a more productive meeting.

> ### • **Plan ahead.**

Even in those cases, though, a little thoughtful preparation beforehand will alleviate the need for many of the disruptions. What is not acceptable is standing in protest or walking out in disagreement (more on that under Rule #8).

> ### • **Be rational.**

Having someone out of a seat and up on the table is also generally not accepted practice either. You may laugh, but I would not have written it if I hadn't seen it from the *man in charge* trying to convince us that he was, in fact, *in charge*. Perhaps his message would have been better communicated and received had he remained dignified and seated behind his large oak desk instead of perched up on top of it. Oddly enough, no one was disputing the fact that he was in charge.

> ### • **Be a people person.**

The converse to this problem is those who are prone to remain in their seats long after the meeting has adjourned. These days, far too many folks are content to remain seated at their desks, hiding behind a computer and keyboard. Leadership by e-mail has replaced leadership by walking around as a norm. Too many of us never meet or get to know the people on the other end of our e-mails, even though they are quite often in the same building. As humans we tend to interact better and go an extra mile or two for someone we actually know, with whom we exchange friendly greetings, laugh and joke, and share family stories. On the other hand, when our request is just another short e-mail or phone call—just another faceless somebody asking for something from a faceless someone— it's extremely easy for the faceless someone to type back to the faceless somebody: Request denied—too busy—try later.

During the meeting it is generally good to remain seated. When the meeting is over it is generally bad to remain seated all the time.

The trick is knowing when to remain seated and when to walk around. So when the meeting is over, get up and get out!

#6 No Destroying Fort Property

A generation or so ago parents taught their children to respect the property of others. Kids were warned to stay out of the neighboring yards unless invited in. They were punished or required to make restitution if they broke or damaged something that belonged to someone else. People respected the property of others because they respected other people. This is increasingly not the case.

```
•   Be respectful.
```

Respecting others and their property goes far beyond simply not destroying their things. It means looking out for them and their well-being. It means considering how your actions will affect others. Personal gain should never be made at the expense of someone else. Respecting people and their property is obvious when it comes to their homes, land, vehicles, etc.— the big stuff. Sometimes, though, we take the "what's mine is mine and what's yours is mine" attitude in a not so obvious way. It is entirely too easy to accept credit for the work, ideas, or intellectual property of someone else when the boss thinks we are responsible for a successful project. Next time, try deflecting the credit to the ones around you. Call particular achievements of specific people to the boss's attention. Synergistic cooperation becomes more of a reality and less a buzzword when people realize they are, in fact, part of a team and are getting the respect and credit they deserve.

Lack of respect towards others will do more than destroy property. It will destroy organizations, teams, companies, and personal relationships. Property can be fixed or replaced. An organization that relies on interpersonal relationships often cannot be repaired once the damage is done. Respect goes in all directions: boss to employee, employee to boss, worker to co-worker, friend to friend, husband to wife, wife to husband, child to parent, parent to child, provider to customer, customer to provider, and so on.

> • **Earn the respect of others.**

One more item to note: true respect does not come free or easily. There is a basic respect we owe each other as human beings—the kind of respect that keeps us from destroying or taking someone else's property. Beyond that, respect must be earned. Some of the basic qualities that garner respect are honesty, integrity, sincerity, initiative, loyalty, patience, candor, tact, punctuality, dependability, courage, decisiveness, unselfishness, and faithfulness.

The qualities that earn the respect of others are the same qualities that make great leaders. So, whether a person aspires to be a true leader or is satisfied being one of the crowd, it's developing virtuous qualities that makes an individual worthy of respect.

#7 No Shouting During a Meeting

Sometimes *how* you say something carries more weight than *what* you actually say. The tone of a message is often as important, if not more so, than the content of the message. Shouting, yelling, or even raising your voice in a contentious manner may indicate a loss of self control (which we covered under Rule #4). There's no quicker way to put another person on the defensive than to use an accusatory tone. Carefully chosen words (see Rule #9) conveyed in the right tone go a long way toward accomplishing the desired purpose.

> • **Always consider the *way* you say something.**

The appropriate tone will depend on the circumstances and the content of the message. "I'm sorry you did not receive the promotion" should not be conveyed in a happy-go-lucky tone. Leaders, spouses, and friends occasionally find it necessary to convey unpleasant messages. Maybe you need to inform someone of bad news or an annoying habit (as discussed under Rule #3). Does the tone convey sincerity, warmth, and a genuine desire to continue and improve upon the relationship, or is it cold, indifferent, or condescending? How will the person on the receiving end of the message walk away from the conversation?

Though less obvious, voicemail, letters, and e-mail all carry a tone. Unlike face-to-face conversation, though, the tone in these means of communication is much more difficult to interpret. How many times have you seen a huddle in an office hovering over an e-mail with someone asking, "What do you think he really means?" Most of the time the recipient is not questioning the definition of the words on the monitor. He is trying to interpret the *way* the message was conveyed.

Is the sender angry, stressed, pressed for time, or just rude, demeaning, and obnoxious? In the e-mail world we tend to type out a note in a few moments and fire it off as quickly as possible. The extremely conscientious among us will actually run the spell check before pressing "send." How many feathers have been ruffled and how many pots stirred because the tone of an e-mail conveyed antagonism when the originator had no such intention? In cases like these the author needs to spend the extra time reading and re-reading carefully crafted words with the understanding that the intended audience does not have the benefit of reading his mind—before pressing "send." If there is a possibility the reader will take the words of the message in the wrong vein, it does not hurt to toss in a few extra sentences explaining your purpose, even though that explanation may seem like stating the obvious—obvious to the sender, that is.

Do you see the affect that adding: "I'm not trying to tell anyone how to do their jobs here, I just want to avoid confusion and ensure we are all on the same page. By the way, thanks for all your hard work on this. Please let me know if I'm missing anything. I really appreciate everyone's effort on this project," would have if appended to: "I thought Jim would have the report done by Thursday and I expect Mary to brief the board first thing Monday morning."

> - **Place equal importance on the *way* you say something as you do on *what* you say.**

Sometimes the context of a message calls for a stern tone, as when a boss informs an employee of a need to improve performance. Other times the appropriate tone will be one of encouragement. Occasionally the situation calls for a little humility. The content of the message and the circumstances will dictate the appropriate tone. The important thing is to say what you mean in the manner or tone you intend your message to be received.

#8 Do Not Run Off Without Permission

When children do not get their way they will take their ball and go home. Grown-ups don't get off so easily. Most of us who walk out on a job walk away from a paycheck; military members get thrown into the brig; still others may face serious lawsuits. Walking out on a marriage may end the marriage, but it will also be the beginning of more problems. (NOTE: Anyone in an abusive relationship should *run*, not walk, to professional help!) Except in extreme cases, running off seldom makes any situation better.

Have you ever seen someone walk out of a meeting in protest or disagreement? What was solved? Usually nothing. You cannot make your point, air your grievance, or argue your cause when you are running away.

> **• Face your problems.**

In the short term, running from problems can seem much easier than facing them head on. Many of us go to great extremes to avoid any type of conflict at all, even if it means ignoring a problematic situation instead of dealing with it.

Disappointment is another opportunity for withdrawal. We can be disappointed by jobs, rejection, failed aspirations, even other people. Wounds fester if not treated. Treat the wound quickly and thoroughly, and the healing begins immediately. We must face adverse situations by first analyzing the problem, then determining the desired outcome, then formulating a plan to achieve that outcome. This might mean facing people in uncomfortable circumstances. It might mean asserting yourself tactfully before a problem becomes insurmountable.

Dealing with disappointment can be tough because the disappointment itself seems to drain the energy and motivation we need to face our problems. There are times when no pep talk in the world will make a difference, and each new disappointment seems to breed another, even when all attempts at rational thought should convince us that things are not as bad as we're making them out to be in our minds. Disappointment like this leads to depression. When you try to run away from depression, you only run deeper into it. To deal with the problem, you need to face it. Seek professional counseling if necessary, but admit the problem and face it. The longer you run from it, the more difficult it becomes. Dealing with disappointment and facing your problems requires action—even some small amount of action where visible progress toward a tangible goal can be made in short but regular intervals. The goal itself should be part of a larger plan. The first step may be as simple as determining to talk to someone with whom you've had a disagreement, or as monumental as deciding upon a new career field later in life.

In both cases, and in all those in between, your expectations need to be realistic. If they are not, you only set yourself up for further disappointment. Determine to make progress. Analyze your progress and re-evaluate the situation. Prepare yourself for setbacks. Don't expect that everything you try will work perfectly or turn out better than you had hoped, but celebrate when it does.

Stepping back to observe and analyze a situation is not the same as running away. In fact, you need to take an objective look before you can attack it with any hope for success. Each problem successfully faced makes it that much easier to deal with the next one. So, the next time you're tempted to run off away from a problem, objectively assess your situation and run toward it instead.

#9 Do Not Be Rude, Talk Back, or Say Bad Words

The tongue has been compared to the rudder of a ship; though it is comparatively small in size it sets the course for something far greater than itself. Great leaders have used great words to accomplish great things. Much lesser men have used far lesser words to tear down individuals and organizations. How many great things were never accomplished because some naysayer dismissed an idea before it got off the ground when a little encouragement was all that was really needed?

> • **Choose your words carefully; once spoken they can never really be taken back.**

This is not to say that all negative words are rude or designed to hurt or destroy. Wise counsel can be positive or negative. There are ways to tell a person that he or she is off base, out of line, or headed down a wrong path without condescending, back-talking, chiding, mocking, or destroying ambitions. It's called *tact*. Tact is telling someone he is acting idiotically without calling him an idiot. Tact is informing people they are doing stupid things without calling them stupid.

Snippiness is out-and-out rudeness. It's letting people know you have a Rolex but won't give them the time of day. It is arrogance perfected. Snippiness ensures that others are aware of your superiority (or rather, your self-perception of your superiority). It's letting them know that if anything is done, it will only be done on your terms, and that you will not be nice to deal with.

Gossip and backstabbing are other forms of rude speech that require no explanation, and would be greatly diminished if there weren't so many eager listeners.

Then there are those who have mastered the use of profanity, which does not always bode well for the listener. The fact is, it takes some people three times longer than it should to get through an expletive-reinforced sentence. This in turn keeps many of us watching the second hand tick by as we wait to get a word in edgewise. Even then, only after mentally deleting the extraneous words are we able to process what has just been said. Some people pass off such bawdy language as a bad habit or say, "That's just who I am." Exercise a bit of discipline and self-control, and watch your language. It pays big dividends.

A few carefully chosen words are far better than a tirade of curses and hateful, rude speech. Even the most intelligent people will not be perceived as such when their speech is interlaced with profanity.

Words have meaning. So, say what you mean, and mean what you say. Speak to encourage and edify others, and inspire them to live up to their potential.

#10 Behave at All Times

The final rule is the perfect summary of the other nine. In our society, taking responsibility for our own actions is not popular. We're always looking for someone else to blame. Even the best political apologies start out, "If I have offended anyone...," magically transferring the guilt of the most insensitive, hateful words and actions onto others for their misunderstanding of the *true* intentions.

> • **Follow the Golden Rule: Treat others as you desire to be treated by them.**

All this would be easily avoided if we only considered others first and contemplated the results of our words or actions before letting them fly. Proper behavior requires some amount of discipline, some sense of the fact that *I am not alone on this planet, and the world does not revolve around me.*

But what about the need to retaliate against the "he started it" argument? Apply the rule. Don't lower yourself to bad behavior. In the end, the high ground always wins. Our problem here is that we tend to be shortsighted. We don't want to let anyone get the better of us or make us look bad in the here and now. A life of consistent good behavior is just that: a lifetime investment. We all love to root for the silver screen hero who is constantly hindered by the dirty tricks of his enemies, but never lowers himself to their level of moral poverty, and in the end comes out on top.

Good behavior does not mean letting others take advantage or walk all over you. Good behavior is dealing with those situations in a moral, mature, professional manner, in a way that attracts the admiration of even those who disagree with you.

For our silver screen hero the end comes two and a half hours after the lights dim—not instant gratification, but close. For those of us who live in the real world, though, behaving at all times is a lifelong endeavor, one worth a little effort every single day.

This Document Has Been Signed By:

_____

Buying In

What made the fort rules work for the kids in the fort was the fact that they all bought in or agreed to live by them. They all appended their names to the rules of their own accord—no one coerced them into that agreement. They recognized the need for order in order to make progress (with whatever it is that kids do in a fort). These children ranged in age from six to twelve, and while they could not have expressed it in terms such as "buying in," that is precisely what they did in agreeing to live and work together in harmony, if only during the short period of a fort meeting.

We're not talking about surrendering individual freedoms for the collective good of the state here. We are talking about controlling childish impulses to yell, shout, boss, threaten, throw objects, run away, or be destructive or obnoxious. For certain set periods of time, these kids agreed to live by a set of guiding principles that most of us mature grown-ups would do well to emulate from time to time, if not all the time.

What made the fort rules work was not the rules themselves, but the buy-in. This was, in a microcosm, a government of the people, by the people, for the people, and at some level, the kids understood that. They saw the fort rules as being beneficial to them as a group, and they agreed to act in a civilized manner just to get along.

So then, why can't we all just get along? Maybe we can agree in principle that the fort rules are beneficial to everyone. Certainly we can all agree that no single person has the power, authority, or capability to require the rest of us to abide by the rules. No, each person must buy in individually. Keeping childish thoughts, words, and actions in check requires individual diligence. Without an inward desire to consciously treat others with dignity and foster the interpersonal relationships in our lives, we will go on like unruly children at the playground.

Epilogue

In the end, some people are just unreasonable (they've probably not read this book); the more reasonably you act toward them, the more unreasonable they prove themselves to be.

• **Maintain the high ground.**

The kids in this book built a fort. What are you building? In the grown-up world, we build companies, networks, friendships, and marriages. At the heart of each of these is interpersonal relationships. That's what the *Fort Rules* are all about.

THE END

Now go out
&
Play Nice !

Rules

*1 Obey leader at all times

*2. No Bossing higher positions

*3. No pestering or threatining

*4. No throwing objects (unless at wa~~

*5. Stay in seats at all times durin~
a meeting

*6. No ~~d~~estroying Fort property

*7. No shouting during a meeting

*8. Do Not run off without permissio~

*9. Do Not be ~~no~~rude talkback or

say bad words

10. Behave at all times

This Document has been
signed by: Zachary

Mykaila, Rachel, Jacob and

Hannah.

Thought you might
like this, copied
from "The Fort Book"

So Now What?

Maybe you've bought in to the idea that the Fort Rules are good, at least in theory. But how does one begin to apply them in everyday relationships? The following section is included to get you started. This section is just a stepping-stone. We've given you the Fort Rules. What you do with them from this point is up to you.

Take time to work through the personal assessment questions. You likely noticed that the Fort Rules, as written by the children, are mostly worded in a negative way—"don't do this" and "none of that." In this section we've simplified each rule to its positive implication—a trait worth developing.

Be honest with yourself in your answers. We're not coming to check your homework.

My Secret Fort Book

Personal Application
Rule #1 Lead by Inspiration

Who looks to me for leadership?

For whom am I officially or legally responsible? (These people could be subordinate co-workers, children (for a parent, guardian, or teacher), scouts, or a team if you're a coach.)

Who comes to me for guidance, answers, or advice?

What style of leadership bests suits or describes me?

__ Authoritarian   __Coach

__ Supportive   __ Delegative

__ Other _____

What are my favorite books on leadership? (Don't have any?
Check your local library, bookstore, or on-line source.)

In what ways can I be intimidating? (Be specific and rethink
these actions.)

In what ways could I inspire others? (Be specific and resolve to
take these actions.)

Personal Application
Rule #2 Be Tactful

To whom do I answer? Who is my boss?

Do I volunteer for someone or an organization with a designated leader?

How do I react when I disagree with these people? (Include spouses or significant others—we all answer to them in one way or another.)

Do people respond favorably to my disagreements, or do I tend to make matters worse?

Do we disagree peaceably and work out the issues, or do our disagreements create animosity?

What are specific disagreements in my relationships or specific changes I am seeking right now?

How can I persuade the other person(s)? (Consider finding points of agreement before discussing differences of opinion.)

Personal Application
Rule #3 Be Kind

What are some of the things people do that annoy me?

Have I ever attempted to inform anyone of an annoying habit?

What approach did I take?

What was the response?

Could I use a different approach with a better result?

Has anyone ever informed me of my annoying habits?

What other things do I do that might annoy other people?

Which is more important to me, my habit or the relationship?

How might I improve the situation?

Personal Application
Rule #4 Exercise Self Control

How do I act when I'm upset?

Do I think clearly when I'm frustrated, or do I blame others for the situation?

Do I lose control over my emotions?

Do I lose control over my actions?

What techniques have I tried in these situations to prevent loss of control (breathe deep and count to ten)?

What can I do now to maintain better self control next time I'm angry or upset?

Personal Application
Rule #5 Be Attentive and Courteous

Do I adequately prepare for meetings or other events that require my full attention?

OR am I disruptive during meetings or other formal events? Be honest.

What actions could I take to minimize the disruptions?

Do I have a real relationship with my co-workers, or do I "hole up" in my office or cubicle?

When there is an option of e-mail, phone, or face-to-face conversation, which do I normally choose?

Is that decision affected by the nature of the message and how well I know the other person?

Make face-to-face conversation a part of each day. Get to know the other people at work or your other regular gatherings, especially those you do not normally talk to.

Personal Application
Rule #6 R.E.S.P.E.C.T.

Am I careful to respect the people around me?

Do I use respectful terms or titles when addressing them?

Do I help myself to other peoples' things?

If I make regular withdrawals from the community candy dish, do I make frequent deposits as well?

How would I rate myself on each of these "respectable" qualities?

5 = I'm great!

1 = I need help ☹

__ honesty   __ integrity

__ sincerity   __ initiative

__ loyalty   __ patience

__ candor   __ tact

__ punctuality   __ courage

__ decisiveness   __ unselfishness

__ dependability   __ faithfulness

*You may want to use this list multiple times to evaluate yourself in the many different relationships of your life.

Personal Application
Rule #7 Consider the WAY You Say Something (Before You Say It)

Do I ever stop to think about the *way* I communicate?

Have I ever been hurt or offended by someone else's tone toward me?

Has anyone (since my mother) ever become upset with me for my "tone of voice?" (NOTE: Don't discount your mother's insights—she is probably wiser that you might want to admit.)

How could I have handled the situation differently?

<u>e-mail</u>

Do I run spell check?

All the time?

Do I re-read my e-mail (before sending) to catch the errors spell check misses (i.e., there, their, & they're)? And to ensure the message will come across the way I intend it to?

Do I get a second opinion on e-mails or letters when the message is important, when there is a possibility the message could be taken the wrong way, and if taken the wrong way, the outcome could be disastrous?

Personal Application
Rule #8 Face Your Problems

Do I consider myself confrontational, or would I rather ignore a problem in the hopes it will "just go away?"

Am I suffering from unresolved issues right now?

If so, what are they?

Have I sought counsel? Should I?

For each problem listed, state a desirable outcome and list specific, achievable goals toward that end to get you moving in the right direction.

Don't forget to step back and analyze progress (or lack of it) and adjust your plan as necessary.

Personal Application
Rule #9 Choose Your Words Carefully

How do I feel when I think or find out that others talk about me behind my back?

Do I say things about other people I would be embarrassed for them to hear?

Am I generally kind and polite when speaking to:

__my peers

__my subordinates

__my boss

__my spouse or significant other

__the customer service agent

Am I the mean man or lady children run away from?

Do I curse and swear? A lot? (Particularly in an environment where it's not welcome?)

Time to get the "Swear Jar" out and increase the penalty to a buck-a-word and remember what Mom said, "If you can't say anything nice…"

Personal Application
Rule #10 Behave

What are some attributes I admire in the people with whom I have a relationship (particularly regarding the way they treat me)?

What are some objectionable attributes I have observed in people (particularly regarding the way they treated me)?

Which of the lists most reflects the way I act toward them? (Would they agree with that assessment? Ask them, if you dare.)

What are some relationship items or matters you may need to discuss with your family, friends, or co-workers to get you on the same page and improve your relationships?

What's stopping you from taking action now?

The kids in this book built a fort. You're building something, too. You're building a life, and every life is built on a lifetime of relationships.

Now Go Out
&
Play Nice !

About the Author

As the founder and president of Brigade Business Solutions, Richard A. Hollen brought twenty-plus years of military and defense industry experience together to develop a workforce training program designed specifically for the small business owner. While in Iraq, Richard served as the Deputy Principle Assistant Responsible for (Reconstruction) Contracts. As a US Marine he was assigned to infantry, airborne, survival training, and aviation units. Career high points include:

- Leadership, management, and oversight for day-to-day operation of 600-man squadron, including airfield operations, heavy equipment, logistical support assets, supply chain management, and administrative personnel
- Government contract and program management
- Multiple leadership positions in Quality Assurance, Safety, Standardization, and Operations

Richard's MBA is from the Naval Postgraduate School, where he studied business and government contracting. His personal awards include:

- Bronze Star for unparalleled leadership and business acumen during Operation Iraqi Freedom
- Two Meritorious Service Medals for leading contracting and source selection efforts during high volume of competitive procurements; and for unsurpassed leadership and management, dynamic direction, keen judgment, and inspiring devotion to duty

- Air Medal numeral 6 with gold star and combat V for missions during Bosnia and Kosovo campaigns
- Navy Commendation Medal for exceptional leadership and managerial skills
- McClellan Award for Academic Excellence, Leadership, & Contribution to DoD Acquisitions
- Member: Beta Gamma Sigma international honor society for business excellence

Richard resides in Freeport, Maine with his wife, Kendra, and their five children (who, incidentally, are still building forts!).

About the Illustrator

Fort Rules was illustrated by tenth-grade artist, Julia Damion. She has a lifelong interest in art and music and has received awards for scratchboard work, ink drawings, and statewide piano competitions. Other interests include reading, photography, and travel. In drawing the illustrations in this book Julia struck the perfect balance between technically advanced artwork and the stick figures the kids who built the fort might have drawn. I appreciate her talent and effort on this project. Her imagination brought the *Fort Rules* to life. Julia resides in Maine with her parents, brother, four guinea pigs, two dogs, and a cat.

About Brigade Business Solutions, LLC

Brigade Business Solutions, LLC, is a private consulting firm specializing in federal government contracts, providing professional consultant, proposal development or review, and contract management services to small and midsized businesses. Additionally, Brigade Business provides workforce training in a variety of areas such as leadership, management, communication, process improvement, planning, and operations. Contact us at:

Brigade Business Solutions, LLC
PO Box 123
Freeport, Maine 04032
(207) 272-7439

www.brigadebusiness.com

About Fort Rules LLC

Fort Rules, LLC is the interpersonal relationship center of excellence specializing in developing the social skills that lead to success in business, happy productive work environments, and the day-to-day business of life. Fort Rules, LLC offers programs for all ages and circumstances.

ATTN: Corporations, Companies, and HR & Operations Departments

Many companies provide a customized corporate version of Fort Rules to their entire staff alongside their employee handbook. The employee handbook tells employees when to come to work, what to wear, where to park, and how the benefits plan works. Fort Rules Corporate Edition provides common sense guidelines for getting along in the workplace. Studies show that one of the main reasons for employee dissatisfaction with the workplace is not getting along with co-workers. Fort Rules establishes common ground upon which to develop a harmonious workplace. A pleasant atmosphere doesn't just happen on its own. Inviting offices happen by design. Make the Fort Rules Corporate Edition the beginning of an exciting new workplace, the place where everyone wants to come to work!

Contact us at:

Fort Rules, LLC
PO Box 123
Freeport, Maine 04032
(207) 400-9202

Coming Soon:
Look for

Fort Rules for Kids

Check out
www.fortrules.com
for events, information,
and more!

Notes

Notes

Notes

Notes

Notes

Notes

Notes

www.ingramcontent.com/pod-product-compliance
Lightning Source LLC
Chambersburg PA
CBHW031237280526
45784CB00004B/1610